CONTENTS

- ***Chapter- :*** Powerful tips and tricks to crack any interview.

- ***Chapter-2***: How to wash out the stress.

- ***Chapter-3***: Common interview mistakes

- ***Chapter-4***: Top 100 questions with answers.

- ***Chapter-5***: Final words of advice

- ***Chapter-6***: How to write a cover letter and Sample cover letters

- ***Chapter-7: How to write an effective resume and Sample resumes***

CHAPTER-1

First of all very very CONGRATULATIONS for your call for the interview….

Without wasting much time, here we go to let you know the:

Tips to crack a job interview successfully

Interviews have always been a nerve racking experience. Everybody gets the jitters when it comes to interviews. Relax! Don't panic. Below are the best tips to help you land your dream job.

What'S your requirements:

Read the job description carefully. It is important to understand what is expected from you and whether you fit in that given profile or not. Analyzing your personal strengths and weakness alongside helps in deciding how well the job suits you and how to approach the interview.

Know the employer

Study about the company where you are appearing for the interview. Know their history, vision and objectives so that you are able to answer questions on it. Research well on their future plans so that you are able to align with your job role and how you can benefit them in the long run.

Prepare all in advance:

You must be prepared for the basic interview questions. Make a list of common interview questions - like your introduction, your hobbies, your interests, why should they hire you, etc. Practice them well before your interview and try to make them interesting!

Be on Time, Be punctual:

You must reach the company on time for the interview. It creates a bad impression if you are late for the interview. Try to reach 10 minutes before the call time. It is an important step towards creating a good first impression.

Dress up well

'Dress to impress' is the key to create and leave a good impression. Wear crisply ironed formals, clean shoes and your hair should be neat and tied up.

Be presentable but don't be too glammed up.

Always be confident

No matter how nervous you are, always look confident. Nobody will want to hire a person who is nervous during the interview, as it creates an impression of inability of the candidate to handle workplace situations.

Honesty is the best policy

Be honest in your responses to interview questions. Lying at any point may back fire in the future.

You are not supposed to know everything, so it is okay to accept it humbly. It's better than giving a wrong response and creating a wrong impression as well.

Update your CV

Your CV is the most important document which sells you to the firm. Keep it updated by adding all your skills and experiences. You must not fake information in your resume. Your CV should not be too verbose and lengthy.

Body language

You are noticed in every way and thus the postures and body language

have a significant weightage during interviews. Do not slouch. Sit straightened make eye contacts during conversations.

Make it a two way conversation by asking questions and clarifying your doubts (if you have any).

Get their opinion

As the interview is about to close, ask the interviewer about how it went and what are the chances of being selected. But do not overdo it. Asking for feedback gives a positive impression of the candidate's keenness towards the job.

CHAPER- 2

How to Wash out the stress and fear.

Here are some tips that will surely help you before any interview:

"Sleepless Nights, Loss of Appetite, Anxiety etc. Don't take me wrong as I am not discussing about some disease but these are the few symptoms of Job Interview Fear or Phobia. Nothing to worry about the same, these are very common and during research it was observed that approx. 80% of candidates suffer from Interview Fear / Phobia. At the same time those who overcome the fear of interview, have very high probability of being successful. There are some tips and tricks which can help u in getting your dream job.

Let's find out how to overcome fear of interview & some useful Tips to Crack Job Interview:

1. *Overcome the Fear of Rejection / Losing:*

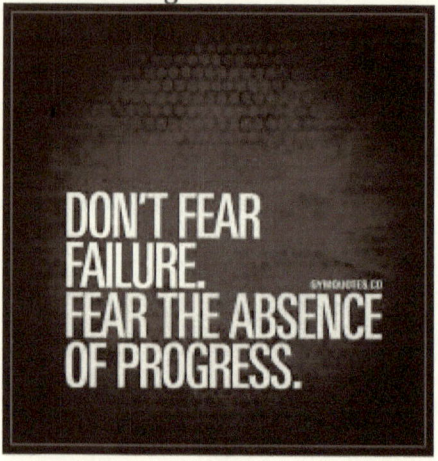

Firstly let's understand why we fear the interview, answer is very simple. It's not fear of interview but fear of rejection so it is very important to overcome the fear of rejection. How can we overcome the fear of rejection?

It is very easy to handle this fear, by simply changing your attitude and approach towards interview. Self-confidence is very important in regard. I am going to share success mantra "Always appear in Interview with attitude as in you don't need this job" YES, you read it right. Always appear in interview with this attitude. This approach will boost your Self Confidence. As per some psychological researches, if we need something in life then we chase it. When we chase, we fear losing it even before getting it. .First focus should be to achieve that particular objective, once you achieve then only fear of losing comes into picture. So appear in interview with Full Confidence and with an Attitude that you don't need this job. It will help you to overcome the fear of rejection or losing the job. No company will hire fearful person so overcome your fear if want the Job.

1. *Understand Job Requirement:*

It is very important to understand what job profile is and whether you fit in this profile or not. Always ask for Job Description before appearing for interview. Identify your strengths & be clear on what kind of candidate organization is looking for. It will help you to decide your approach during course of interview.

2. What all you are bringing it to the table?

Always think that if you need this particular job then at the same time, organization is also looking for a good candidate.

During interview always focus on what all skill sets you will bring to organization & how it will benefit the organization in long benefit. Job is also doing a business, in our daily life if we buy any product or hire any service. We always look how this product or service will benefit us similarly you are also doing business with organization and try to showcase how organization is going to benefit if they offer this job to you.

3. *Probable Questions & Answers:*

Once you are clear on Job Requirement, make a list of probable questions and their answers i.e. what all an interviewer can ask you. If need arises take help of your friends who are in similar position or industry. Trust me if you do this exercise seriously, you will be able to find out at least 80% of questions which can be asked during the interview

4. *Never Fudge or fabricate your CV:*

It's a biggest and most common mistake by most of candidates. My sincere advice never ever fudge your CV. Organizations are smart & they will find out very easily that you have fabricated your CV. It can create problem for u in future and can even spoil your career, so always be honest in your approach.

5. *Never Argue with Interviewer:*

It is advisable not to enter into any kind of argument with Interviewer during interview. Let's accept that the person who is taking the interview has more experience, just listen & don't argue to justify your point. I am not saying don't put across your point but put it in a positive manner & don't argue to justify that you are correct

6. *Be Honest & Flexible:*

Always be honest during interview. If u don't know any answer just accept the same rather trying to give wrong answers. Besides knowledge, organizations give lot of importance to people who are honest in approach and also flexible in their approach. Never be rigid in your approach as business environment is changing very fast these days. Organizations always give importance to people with flexible approach rather rigid in nature.

8. Ask for feedback at the end of Interview:

Before the interview closes, ask for feedback from interviewer irrespective how your interview went. It gives very positive impression about candidate. Organization feels that candidate has positive attitude & is willing to accept feedback

9. *Salary Negotiations:*

Never ever ask for unrealistic salary hikes as it gives impression that you are not serious about the job and just changing the job for money. Kindly do your homework before salary negotiation i.e. with your experience and for the particular job profile what is industry benchmark. For junior and middle management, normal salary hike is in the range of 25% to 40%. Also in some of critical job profiles like treasury in banking you might get very high salary hike.

10. *Never ditch the organization after accepting the Job:*

Again very common mistake and some people have habit of keep trying in various organizations for better package after receiving job offer & if they get another job, they simply say NO before joining. Trust me it can spoil your career in long run and you will never be able to reach top management with this attitude. World is very small and in this networked age you can't hide these kind of actions. In future you will again come across same people & then no one will hire, if they find that you indulged in these tactics. If you don't wish to join then please don't accept offer letter but after accepting if you say NO then it is totally unethical and unprofessional.

CHAPTER -3

Common Interview Mistakes that Could Cost You Your Dream Job (and How to Avoid Them)

There have been many articles you would have already read but here we want to help our readers as much as we can.

Now, we will look at the 5 common interview mistakes that could cost us our dream job and how to avoid them.

We are not going to go into the obvious interview red flags- dressing sloppy, not being on time, not carrying a copy of your resume or identification when you were told to, etc. We are all better than that, right? This is more about the answers to some common interview questions that might come out wrong.

1. *Negativity:*

No complaints about your past. This might happen when answering questions like "Why are you looking for a change?" We can very easily say something 'not nice' about our previous work experience.

> *For e.g.*
>
> *A small anecdote: My first job was with a major Indian IT consulting firm and I being an entry-level fresher, I was a buffer/shadow/non-billable resource in a testing project. I was not given any real work and all I had to do was "learn" by watching. My job was simply to consolidate all the bug reports created by the individual testers in the team at the end of the day. Trust me, it was pathetic. But, that's not the point.*

Say, this is the position you are trying to make a move from. When a question comes to you- "What was your role in the project?" What is your answer going to be? There are two ways to handle this- the optimist and the pessimist way.

The pessimist way is to complain how you were not trusted with any important tasks and all you had to do was merge the individual bug reports. The optimist way is to explain how you were the quality representative for your team who made sure the bug reports were complete and had no duplicates/inaccurate information – or how you got a chance to look into the entire project related issues and in effect the entire project instead of being confined to a certain module. It is apparent which one is a better answer, correct?

So, no matter how bad the current job/company/boss/salary/project/process – it helps to find what is good about them and only choose that part to include in your answers during an interview.

2. *Lying about your skills on the resume:*

This is an aspect that cannot be reminded enough. We all want good jobs, we all want our resumes to be noticed and more than that, we want that lifeless-resume-search-engine to pick just us from all the 1000s of them out there. This often leads to a kind of passive desperation and compels us to put something on our resume that isn't totally correct. E.g. adding automation tools when you don't have any hands-on experience. We might successfully fool the machine, but we won't be able to do that with an interviewer. Careful what you write in there.

3. *Talking endlessly:*

Another personal experience to share here. There was this one interview a few years ago when I almost had the job. It was a referral, a perfect fit to my skill set and the interview panel had a few of my friends. I still did not get the job. Frankly, I would not have hired myself. Why? I would not stop talking and I had no idea what I was talking. The very same day, I came back from an international business trip, was jet-lagged and sleep-deprived- Traveled way too far on a hot summer afternoon in the busy city traffic and was out of breath when I got there. So, when the interviewer asked me questions, I was all about 'just talking' instead of saying anything meaningful. I learnt that day when we can't be "Present" we should not be. So, when you have an interview and you are serious about making it successful- be present, answer only appropriately and be professional. If you can't be – respectfully reschedule.

Other common interview mistakes in conversational are:

Trying to use big words out of context: This will cause unnecessary follow up questions. Say, you have no idea but have heard about "Business continuity plan- BCP". When you were asked about test planning, you said we also have to come up with a BCP- but not knowing the full extent on the topic. The interviewer, as expected, will ask you what BCP is and the rest, I don't have to explain.

Filler words: There are a few filler words we use often-mostly when nervous- in conversations. One of my trainers always used the phrase "The one" and I have been told that I say "So" very often to keep the flow of a sentence going. Recognize if that's happening and try to stay calm. It's ok to be nervous, but the real trick is to camouflage it. Think of an interview as a professional conversation – listen and respond appropriately.

4. Do not commit:

Commit to working hard. Commit to integrity. Commit to discipline. But do not commit to a timeline, salary expectation or anything more serious. Let me give you an example, how long will you stay with the company? – try to say something non-committal- "as long as it takes (with a smile)" or "however long you would like me to stay" are all good because you are not promising anything. If you say- "As long as I find it challenging" – this will mean, you will quit the minute work is more routine. "As long as it is good for my career"- means you are only interested in your welfare and do not care about the company. Really, there is no good way to answer questions like this- So, invite your sense of humour and stay on a neutral ground.

5. *What are your weaknesses?*

Wait, don't answer that. We are human, thus- not perfect. Also, we know our weaknesses best. It does not mean we have to go about letting everyone know of them. Especially not in an interview. Twist the answer around to mean that it is strength of yours. You can say "You can't stand grammatical/spelling errors in reference documents"- this will mean you are diligent and want things to be in a standard way. Or you can say- "I often arrive at meetings early and have to wait for the others, which can be quite annoying"- shows punctuality. So, you get the picture, right?

Well, we hope we have conditioned you (just kidding) to spot these interview red flags early on and to avoid the danger.

CHAPTER -4

Top 100 Common Job Interview Questions

Job interviews are a key part of the hiring process. They can also be incredibly nerve-wracking! The best way to calm any pre-interview jitters is to prepare well-crafted responses to the major questions coming your way.

While you can't predict exactly what the hiring manager will ask you, you can come up with answers to the most common questions. This guide contains the top 100 questions that hiring managers ask in a job interview.

Before getting to the list, let's consider why it's so important to prepare for job interview questions, rather than just winging it.

Why Should You Prepare for Job Interview Questions?

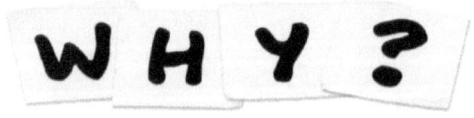

Interviews are important; there's no getting around that. They're often your first opportunity to communicate directly with a hiring manager and advocate for yourself as the best person for the job.

While some interviews are more conversational than others, none of them feel like the most natural social dynamic. The interviewer's going to ask you some open-ended, some specific questions about your skills and experiences, and you should be prepared to answer them in a strategic way. The last thing you want to do is go blank or start rambling about your childhood dog.

To excel in your interview, you should prepare your responses to common interview questions. With enough mock interview practice leading up to the real thing, you can make sure your answers sound natural and leave an excellent impression.

For more on how to answer common interview questions, check out our guide with tips and sample responses! For now, let's go over how this list of 100 questions is sorted into categories.

"How Does This List Work?"

No interviewer's going to ask you 100 questions in a row unless they possess King Joffrey levels of cruelty. However, they might sample a few questions from each of the below categories to get a full sense of your skills and experiences. There are five categories of questions in this list:

- ✓ **traditional,**
- ✓ **behavioral,**
- ✓ **cultural fit,**
- ✓ **logistical,**
- ✓ **and curveballs.**

Traditional questions are the ones with which you might already be familiar. They tend to be open-ended and ask about your background, goals, and work style.

Behavioral questions are some of the trickiest, because they ask you to provide specific examples that illustrate an achievement, a learning experience, or even a failure.

Cultural fit questions are also common, and they're particularly important for organizations that place high value in workplace culture. These may feel more personal or creative, but your answers should still be tailored to the organization at hand.

Logistical questions tend to focus on your work history, how long you plan to stay, and salary expectations.

Curveball questions are the random ones that you might expect during an icebreaker on your first day of summer camp. Don't dismiss these questions as unimportant, though, as they're an opportunity to let your personality shine through. Curveball questions can also be another way that the manager gauges cultural fit.

You'll find 99 questions sorted into these five categories. As for the special 100th question? That one's at the end of the list, and it's a virtually universal question that every interviewee must be prepared to answer!

Before getting to that final essential question, plus some extra tips on how to prepare, let's start in with some of the most common traditional job interview questions.

The **"tell me about yourself"** prompt is an old classic, like apple pie at Thanksgiving.

Don't be surprised if your interviewer brings it to the table.

Traditional Questions:

Who Are You? What Are Your Qualifications for the Job?

The questions in this category are fairly common interview questions that interviewers have been asking for years. They're often some of the first questions in an interview that get the conversational ball rolling as the interviewer explores your professional skills, attitudes, and experience.

Common Traditional Job Interview Questions:

1. Tell me about yourself.

2. What do you consider to be your greatest professional strengths?

3. What would you say are your weaknesses?

4. Why do you want this job?

5. Why should we hire you?

6. What would you contribute to this job?

7. If you had a personal mission statement, what would it be?

8. If you had to describe yourself in one word, what would it be?

9. What do you feel makes you unique?

10. What do you find motivating?

11. How do you define and measure success?

12. Where do you see yourself in five years?

13. How does this position fit in with the career path you see for yourself?

14. Would you consider yourself a big-picture person or a detail-oriented person?

15. What are some of your hobbies?

16. What were some responsibilities in your previous job?

17. What's your work style like?

18. What were some of your favorite things to do in your last position?

19. What were some of your least favorite things to do in your last job?

20. What would your manager say are your best strengths?

21. What would your manager say are areas that you need to develop more?

22. How do you make decisions?

23. What could you contribute to make this company better?

24. What are you looking for in your next position?

25. What's your style of management?

26. Can you describe the best boss you ever had?

27. Can you describe the worst boss you ever had?

28. How do you manage your time?

29. What are you looking for regarding career development?

30. What's a goal you have for self-improvement in the next year?

31. How has your education gotten you ready for your career?

32. If you got this job, what would some of your goals be?

33. How do you keep yourself organized?

34. Do you prefer working in a team or alone?

❖ *Answering Traditional Questions:*

As you can see, traditional questions tend to ask about your skills and what you would bring to the job. While some of the questions may sound more personal, like "tell me about yourself" or "what makes you unique?" they're all openers to advocate for your professional qualifications.

Your answers, therefore, should be tailored to the job and organization. A common mistake is to talk only about your own goals and what you're looking for in a new job. While a hiring manager does want to see your motivations and passions, she's also concerned with making a successful hire. She needs to see not just what you want, but what you could do for her organization.

As you prepare your responses, then, you should consider the job description and what the company seeks. If one of the core competencies, or main skills, of the job is teamwork and collaboration, then you probably shouldn't start talking about how much you prefer to work alone. You should bring in the core competencies of the job in your responses, albeit in a natural-sounding way.

In addition to tailoring your responses, a second tip for answering these questions is bringing in specific examples. Who doesn't like to hear a good story? Even if the question doesn't ask for a specific example, you could often benefit from sharing one, especially if you're someone who tends to drift into vague language. To make your answers more concrete, you could pinpoint particular instances from your past.

The next category, **behavioral questions**, explicitly asks you to bring in specific examples. Unless you're a pro at thinking on your feet, these can be some of the most difficult questions to answer on the spot. Luckily, you'll be prepared with your examples before you walk in the door!

Interviewers ask behavioral questions so that you'll give specific examples of times that you succeeded, handled conflict, or, like this tired corkscrew, went above and beyond the call of duty.

Behavioral Questions: How Do You Act on the Job?

As someone who struggles to come up with a specific example when put on the spot, I think behavioral questions are pretty much the worst. At the same time, they're also super common. Chances are, you'll get asked a bunch of behavioral questions in your job interview.

Hiring managers don't just want to hear abstract ideas about your work ethic or skills. They want to hear about specific times when you achieved something, managed conflict, or bounced back after a failure.

One rationale for these questions is that past behavior indicates future behavior. By gaining a sense of what you've done in the past, the hiring manager has a clearer vision of how you'll perform in the future.

The other reason behind these questions is that behavioral questions and answers are simply more interesting. They call for specific stories, and these stories make your candidacy more memorable and colorful. You want to leave a great impression, and intriguing anecdotes are one way to accomplish this.

Below you'll find some common examples of behavioral questions, followed by some tips for answering them.

Common Behavioral Questions

35. Can you describe a time you demonstrated leadership?

36. Can you speak to a time that you had to handle criticism of your work?

37. Tell me about a time when your workload was especially heavy and how you dealt with it.

38. What would you do if you were asked to take on more assignments than you could conceivably finish by the expected deadlines?

39. Can you give me an example of a time you had to follow a policy with which you didn't agree?

40. Tell me about a time you went above and beyond expectations at work.

41. Have you ever worked on a time when someone was not pulling his weight? What did you do?

42. Have you ever had trouble working with a manager?

43. Can you tell me about a time your boss disagreed with something you did? How did you deal with it?

44. How do you handle difficult customers?

45. How do you deal with stressful situations?

46. Have you ever had to deal with a coworker who put you down at work? What did you do?

47. Can you tell me about a time that you faced a difficult situation with a colleague?

48. Give me an example of a time that you failed.

49. Have you ever had to give someone tough feedback? How did you go about that?

50. Have you ever gone against official policy or directives? Why? What were the results?

51. Can you give me an example of a challenge or conflict you faced at work? Describe how you handled it.

❖ Answering Behavioral Questions

As you can see, behavioral questions explicitly ask you to give specific examples. Your mission, then? To highlight success stories that show you possess some of the core competencies the interviewer is looking for.

Just as all your answers should be tailored to the job at hand, so too should your examples be chosen based on the job description and organization. If problem-solving is a big part of the prospective job, then chooses an example, if possible, that demonstrates your problem-solving skills.

Similarly, if you're asked to provide a failure, don't choose a story where you failed because you lack one of the core competencies. If the position wants you to be highly organized, don't go on and on about your problems with organization. In fact, you could subtly highlight the opposite; maybe there was a time you failed to look at the big picture because you were too concerned with details of organization, and you've since learned how to balance the two.

As you know by now, you should tailor your responses, but don't just tell the interviewer what you think she wants to hear or choose a cop-out answer, like "I work too hard" or "I care too much." You still want to be authentic and true to yourself.

The best way to ace these behavioral questions is to show up with a few prepared success stories in your mental suitcase. Perhaps you can pack four or five that relate to the most common questions - a time you showed leadership, a challenge you faced, a story about teamwork, an example of problem solving, and an instance of failure.

One final tip about that "describe a time that you failed" prompt - don't focus too much on failure. Be honest about the failure, but show how you saw it as a learning opportunity. Talk about how you acknowledged, addressed, and grew from your mistake. Your attitude toward setbacks may be just as important as the story you share.

Now that you have a sense of those tricky behavioral questions and how to prepare for them, let's look at the next major category: questions that aim to gauge your cultural fit.

Maybe your ideal workplace values teamwork, innovation, or indoor climbing walls. Let the interviewer know what draws you to its culture.

Cultural Fit Questions: Do You Share Our Values?

Organizational culture has always been important for employees, and today it seems to be even more so. Many private companies, in particular, pay a ton of attention to workplace values and the happiness levels of employees. Good morale and workplace perks can improve individual performance, retention, and teamwork, as well as prevent workplace conflict.

Many hiring managers, therefore, will ask interview questions aimed at gaining a sense of your cultural fit. Check out some of the questions below, and then read on for a few tips on how to prepare for them.

Common Cultural Fit Questions:

52. What does teamwork mean to you?

53. What three qualities do you look for in a workplace?

54. How would you deal with a coworker you don't get along with?

55. How well would you say you adapt to change?

56. What are you passionate about?

57. Describe your ideal company culture. What four or five characteristics does it have?

58. Who inspires you and why?

59. What motivates you to come into work everyday?

60. What was it like working at your last company?

61. What are some of your workplace values?

62. Do you prefer a more structured work environment or one where you can be more entrepreneurial?

63. What personality types would you say you work best with?

64. What are some activities you like to do outside of work, and how do they benefit your day-to-day job?

65. What would your friends tell me about you?

❖ **Answering Cultural Fit Questions**

As you can see, a lot of these cultural fit questions focus on workplace values. They also bring out soft skills, like communication, flexibility, motivation, passion, and outside interests.

While these questions are opportunities to let your personality shine through, don't forget that you're in a job interview. You still want to customize your answers to the organization, and the best way to do this is to research its culture online and, if possible, by speaking to its employees. The company website's a great resource, as well as sites like LinkedIn and Glass door. If you know any people who work there, definitely reach out and ask them about their experiences.

These cultural fit questions work two ways. The manager wants to see how you'd fit in, but you also want to make sure the culture aligns with your values and work style. Make sure it's the sort of place you'd like to work and could be successful. Find out about values, and, if you share them, reflect this understanding and alignment in your responses.

Logistical questions might ask about a gap in employment or a career change, such as,

"Going from a dog walker to a NASA astronaut seems like a big change. Could you speak on that a bit?"

Logistical Questions: Employment History and Salary Expectations

Logistical questions tend to be straightforward. They might ask about details on your resume, your professional goals, or your salary expectations. Some of these questions, especially about salary, may show up later in the hiring process, like in a second interview.

You should be prepared to discuss them, though, just in case. Below are some common questions that fall into this logistical category.

Common Logistical Questions

66. You worked at your last company for a long time. Will it be difficult moving to a new firm?

67. Why have you changed jobs so often over the past few years?

68. If you got this job, how long would you plan to stay with us?

69. What did you earn at your last job?

70. What are your salary expectations?

71. Why do you have a gap in your job history?

72. Why do you think you can lead a team without any previous managerial experience?

73. Why do you want to join our company?

74. Why do you want to move from an academic field to the business world (or vice versa)?

75. Why should we give you the job over other applicants?

76. Would you jump ship if you received another offer?

77. What other companies are you applying to?

78. Why did you freelance for a long period of time?

79. What caused you to leave your last position?

80. Why do you want to leave your current position?

81. Why did you take a job that seems unrelated to your career path?

❖ **Answering Logistical Questions**

While you may have already talked about your skills and experiences, these logistical questions will get you talking specifically about your professional history. Be prepared to speak on your last job, its responsibilities, and your reasons for applying elsewhere.

If you have any gaps in employment or are making a career change, you should also be ready to speak on that. As for salary, interviewers may save this question for later in the hiring process, like a second interview. You shouldn't be dishonest about what you've made in the past, but you may decline to share by saying that the two jobs are so different, you don't feel your last salary applies to the current situation.

If you're just not sure, do some research on the company website and sites like Payscale and Glass door to see what you could expect from a comparable position. I've found

these sites sometimes have such a big range it's hard to be sure, but you can look at the available information and then decide what's a reasonable range for you.

Again, as you should in all your responses, make sure to communicate your enthusiasm for the position and commitment to the organization should you be hired.

Finally, let's consider the fifth category of questions, **the curveballs**.

Don't get thrown by random questions, like, "If you were a vacation, would you be a camping trip, a group tour, or a luxury spa?"

Curveball Questions: The Odd and Unexpected

We've reached the quirky curveball questions. Like they sound, these questions run the gambit of total randomness. They tend to be odd and imaginative, and are mainly asked to gain a sense of you. Personality and ability to think on your feet. Of course, if you've already prepared for the right ones, then you won't have to think on your feet!

Some questions aim to root out your entrepreneurial qualities or vision. Others seek to see how you self-reflect and make decisions. Others, well - it's hard to say what some of these are getting at. That's why I decided to call them curveballs!

Check out some potential curveball questions below, along with ten real-life examples that interviewers from big companies, like Drop-box and Trader Joe's have asked prospective employees. Then check out some tips on how to prepare for the unexpected!

Potential Curveball Questions

82. If you could live your life over again from the beginning, what's one thing that you would change?

83. If you could be an animal, which one would you be and why?

84. If you could relive the last 10 years of your life, what would you do differently?

85. If you were a tree, what kind of tree would you be?

86. What's one new thing you taught yourself in the last year?

87. What would the name of your app be?

88. You have two minutes. Teach me something.

89. Why do people climb mountains?

90. From Space Exploration Technologies: When a hot dog expands, in which direction does it split and why?

91. From Whole Foods Market: Would you rather fight 1 horse-sized duck, or 100 duck-sized horses?

92. From Drop-box: If you're the CEO, what are the first three things you check about the business when you wake up?

93. From Urban Outfitters: What would the name of your debut album be?

94. From J.W. Business Acquisitions: How would you sell hot cocoa in Florida?

95. From Hubspot: If I gave you $40,000 to start a business, what would you start?

96. From Trader Joe's: What would you do if you found a penguin in the freezer?

97. From Boston Consulting Group: If you were a brand, what would be your motto?

98. From Delta Air Lines: How many basketballs would fit in this room?

99. From Satish: If you had Rs.2,000, how would you double it in 24 hours?

❖ **Answering Curveballs**

Is it possible to prepare for the unpredictable? Sure, to some extent. While you may not know exactly what questions you'll get asked, you can hone your skills of thinking on your feet.

Improve actors, for example, don't just get up on stage and see what happens. They keep their imaginations active and flexible with improve activities. You might similarly try a rapid-fire question and answer practice session to see what you come up with. You should find that your answers come easier and more creative the more you warm up.

As with all your other answers, you might be able to tailor your responses to the job. For instance, if you get asked about what kind of animal you would be, you could choose one that's associated with leadership, like a lion, cleverness, like a monkey, or strong work ethic, like an ant, depending on what the job's looking for.

At the same time, try not to overthink these too much. They're more lighthearted and chances to reveal your personality and sense of humor. And if you find your mind totally goes blank, you could try to buy a little extra time with the old trick of, "That's a great question. I'll have to think about that for a second."

Now that you've read over 99 common interview questions in the five major categories, let's take a look at the final question that almost every interviewer asks at the end of your meeting.

Even if your interviewer doesn't ask you any of the previous 99 questions, you can be pretty sure that she'll ask you this next one!

Final Crucial Job Interview Question

Finally, you've made it to the end of the list and have seen 99 of the most common traditional, behavioral, cultural fit, logistical, and curveball questions that might come your way in the job interview. But we promised you 100 questions, and saved the nearly universal question for last.

This question is an absolute must for your interview preparation. Almost every interviewer asks it, and there's definitely a way that you can answer it wrong. Here it is:

100. Do you have any questions for me?

❖ **Answering the Final Question**

This final question's not a particularly hard one, but it is very important. The biggest mistake you could make here is to say, "Nope!" The answer to this question should always be yes, and you should have at least two thoughtful questions to ask your interviewer.

You may be sick of reading about how your answers should be tailored to the job and organization at hand, so I'll just say it one last time: your questions should be tailored to the job and organization at hand (sorry).

Your questions are one more opportunity to show your interest and enthusiasm. You can show that you've researched the organization and have a strong understanding of its culture and mission. Don't ask questions that can be easily answered with a Google search. Similarly, don't ask ones that you just talked about ten minutes before.

What you already know about the company can inform your questions, though, as it shows you've done some digging. You might say, "I saw on your website that one of your long-term goals is xyz. Could you tell me about some of the specific steps you'll be taking in the next few months to work toward this?"

You could ask about a typical day in the office, what your team members would be like, or what qualities the company values most in its employees. For more suggestions on questions to ask at the end of your interview, check out this question and answer guide.

So there you have it, one hundred of the most common questions that get asked in job interviews. In closing, let's go over the key pieces of advice to remember as you prepare to rock your job interview.

Here's one piece of advice: Do your preparation before you get to the interview!

CHAPTER -5

Preparing for Interview Questions: Final Words of Advice

Interviews can be an intimidating hurdle in the hiring process, but believe it or not, they can also be exciting! They're your opportunity to speak with your next potential manager and teammate, learn more about an organization, and show that you're the best person for the job.

With enough preparation, you can give succinct, thoughtful responses to any interview question. While you may not be able to completely eliminate all the unknowns, you can definitely reduce them considerably. As you consider how you would answer the above questions, make sure you keep these four main guidelines in mind.

CHAPTER- 6

How to Write a Cover Letter: Full Template

Cover letters are an essential part of your applications. They're often your first opportunity to communicate with a hiring manager and stand out from the crowd.

Because cover letters play such an important role, they can often feel almost impossible to write. To help you break through writer's block, we've put together this comprehensive cover letter template with real examples. Scroll down for the full template, or first check out some tips to guide your thinking.

When Do You Need a Cover Letter?

Cover letters play a key role in the hiring process. Typically, you **send a cover letter along with your resume when you apply to a job.** You might also write one to make a general inquiry about potential opportunities with a company you're interested in. If you're enlisting a headhunter in your job search, then you'll also need to provide a cover letter to help him/her understand your qualifications.

For the purposes of this guide, we'll mainly stick to cover letters that you **send when you're applying to a job.** The general advice, though, applies to all types.

To write an effective cover letter, you need to know what to include and what to leave out. To help guide you through the writing process, I've picked out the **four most important characteristics of a great cover letter.**

What Should a Cover Letter Say?

Cover letters can be challenging because you have to **say a lot in only a few words.** In most cases, your cover letter should just be one page. You have to strive to be concise while describing how your qualifications match up to the new job description. Plus, you want some of your personality to shine through and connect with the reader!

There are several elements to a great cover letter, but I've highlighted the **four most important ones.** When you're writing yours, keep these overarching goals in mind. Your cover letter should accomplish the following:

1. **Focus On What You Can Do for the Employer**

Rather than talking about how great the job would be for *you*, you should instead **focus on what you can bring to the organization.** This might a subtle shift, but it helps you keep your cover letter focused and on point.

Before you start writing, make sure to **deconstruct the job description and investigate the industry.** Gain a clear understanding of the new position and its requirements and express this understanding in your letter. Then you can **analyze your specific skills, knowledge, and qualifications in relation to the job requirements.** Consider both "hard" technical skills and "soft" transferable skills and professional behaviors.

Even if you haven't worked a related job or have jumped around, you can show how your skills would transfer to the role. **Transferable skills** can be just as if not more important than a directly related work history. Present your skills in terms of the contributions you could make and value you could bring to the organization.

Use the STAR framework - Situation, Task, Action, Result - to brainstorm specific examples for your cover letter.

2. Give Specific Examples with the STAR Framework

Your cover letter is an opportunity both to **personalize your application and to differentiate yourself from other candidates.** It shouldn't simply be a repeat of your resume.

To make your letter unique and personal, you should **incorporate a specific example or two of your accomplishments into your letter.** If you focus on your marketing skills, for instance, then you could provide a specific example of an especially effective marketing campaign. If you say you helped students improve their English language skills, then you might add a sentence or two about a student and the activities you implemented to help her learn.

One useful framework for brainstorming specific examples is called the STAR approach. It stands for **Situation, Task, Approach, and Result.** To use this framework, consider a situation you faced or task you were assigned. Then think about what approach you took to address it. Finally, what were your results?

This framework isn't just useful for your cover letters; it's **also a helpful approach when you interview.** It helps take your ideas from the realm of the abstract to the real. Instead of vague descriptions, this framework helps you zero in on specific demonstrations of your skills and experiences. It helps you tell a story about who you are.

3. Communicate Enthusiasm

Now that you have an initial sense of the content of your cover letter, let's talk for a second about tone. Overall, you want your letter to **communicate a strong sense of enthusiasm.**

In many ways, your cover letter is your marketing tool. It communicates your **personal brand**, the bundle of skills, experiences, and behaviors that defines your professional identity. You can use it to reveal some dimensions of your personality. As the best cover letters are highly customized, they should **express excitement about the specific position and**

organization. Often, the most memorable cover letters are the ones with the most personality and enthusiasm.

You might start out by saying how pleased or excited you were to learn about the position or state your great interest in joining the team. Your enthusiasm, as well as the effort you put in to craft a strong letter, should **shine through** your whole cover letter.

4. Be Readable, Clear, and Brief:

Another important, if challenging, feature of your cover letter is its **readability.** Consider the perspective of the hiring manager. They may be pressed for time and reading lots of applications. They want to be able to **get to the heart of what you have to say** without putting in lots of effort. For any Lit majors out there, think Ernest Hemingway rather than James Joyce.

Your letter should **cut to the chase** and present its points in a clear and straightforward way. Aim to be concise and precise. Ultimately, your goal with a cover letter is to say a lot in a few words.

This can be a challenging task, but don't worry - even if your letter starts out wordy and scattered, you can **tighten it up as you edit.** First drafts are supposed to be unpolished. By revising and proofreading, you can bring your cover letter into its best form.

The level of formality might vary by industry. A traditional corporation might look for a more formal letter, while a start-up in a creative industry might want to see something untraditional and conversational. Changing up the style and format can **work in your favor and help you stand out,** but make sure that your writing remains clear, concise, and approachable!

Now that you have an initial sense of what should go into your cover letter, let's take a closer look at the form of the letter itself. First, an **important disclaimer about application instructions.** Then read on for the full cover letter template, explained piece by piece!

Your cover letter's not the time to wander off on tangents. Aim to be clear, concise, and readable.

Disclaimer: Follow Application Instructions

As you just read, there can be a lot of variation among cover letters depending on the job, industry, and your personal style. Another key factor that determines what your cover letter looks like and how you send it is the **application instructions.**

Many jobs will give you certain guidelines, so you should **make sure to abide by them.** They might ask you to apply through a job application portal and paste your cover letter and resume into text boxes. Similarly, they might ask you to paste your cover letter and even resume directly into the body of an email. If this is the case, then you don't have to worry too much about formatting, as this plain text format will largely remove any special features.

On the other hand, you might be instructed or choose to send your letter as a hard copy or a Word attachment. If you attach your letter, then you can just write a brief message in the body of the email telling your reader to check out the attachments. In these **more traditional modes**, you can customize your formatting more.

The instructions might also give you **a word limit or tell you about next steps.** Some jobs explicitly say, "No calls," to make sure the office doesn't get bombarded with communication. Make sure to **read and follow any application instructions as you prepare your materials.** That being said, let's dive into the template to help you guide your cover writing letter from start to finish.

How to Write a Cover Letter: Full Template

At the risk of undermining the template you're about to read, I want to start with a word of caution. Don't follow this template too religiously! The best cover letters are unique and customized. You want to **stand out from the crowd of other applicants**, not blend in and lose your edge.

At the same time, the strongest cover letters typically do have certain features in common. Most start with a strong opener, followed by two to three body paragraphs that **argue for your candidacy.** Finally, they end with an enthusiastic conclusion and your name.

The first part of your letter depends on how you're sending it. You may add a header, or start right in with the salutation, as you'll read below.

1. Choose Your Format

To start your letter, you may add a header or start right in by addressing the hiring manager. Traditionally, cover letters included a header at the top with both your and the hiring manager's contact information. If you're sending a **hard copy of your cover letter or attaching it as a separate Word document**, then this format is a good one to use.

However, many other applicants simply copy and paste their cover letters directly into the body of the email. Other companies use job application portals that ask you to copy and paste your letter into a text box. In these cases, you can **skip the traditional contact information at the top and just start right in with the salutation.**

If you're using a traditional format, then you'd write your name, address, and the current date at the top. You might also include your phone number and email address. Ideally, your header would **match**

the one you use on your resume to give your entire application a cohesive, packaged look. Your letterhead could look something like this:

XYZ
85 Cambridge St.
Cambridge, MA 87161

June 1, 2018

Again, some people also have their **phone number and email** at the top. Others include it at the bottom, after their signature and printed name. Either way is fine, as long as the hiring manager can clearly see how to contact you.

Below the date, you could insert the hiring manager's contact information. Ideally, you can **write to a specific person** who has the power to hire you. If you can't find any specific contact information, then you could just put the company and its address. Here's an example of the contact information for a school principal:

Mr. ABC
School Principal
City Middle School

1 School Road
Cityville, NJ 9868

Below this contact information, you'd start right in on the salutation. Again, if you're pasting your cover letter into an email or text box, then you can **skip all this formatting!**

Truth be told, the format of your cover letter is not a huge deal, and it definitely shouldn't be a deal breaker in the hiring manger's eyes. The **content of your letter is much more important.** Before delving into that content, let's consider the salutation, or how to address your letter.

2. Add a Salutation

Addressing your cover letter can be a source of anxiety for some people. Best practices usually dictate that you should **address your letter to a specific person,** but what if you have no idea who you're writing to?

First off, it really is a good idea to try to address your letter to a specific person. **Try your best to track down the hiring manager** via Google, the organization's website, or LinkedIn. If you can't find the specific person, you might consider writing to the head of the department, if applicable.

If you really can't find anyone, then there's one other potential way to personalize an otherwise anonymous salutation. You could specify the position by writing something like, "Dear Content Manager Search Committee" or "Dear Data Scientist Hiring Manager." These greetings indicate that you're writing with a **specific audience in mind**, even if you don't know who exactly he/she is.

If you can't find any point person, then don't sweat it! You can just write, **"Dear Hiring Manager" or "Dear Hiring Professional."** You should probably steer clear of "To Whom It May Concern," as it's become a bit overused and sounds distant. Likewise, avoid the antiquated "Dear Sirs."

Again, don't worry too much about the salutation. The **content of your cover letter is the part that deserves most of your attention.** So without further ado, let's jump into that content, starting with the introduction.

There are several tried-and-true phrases you can use to start your cover letter. This, however, isn't one of them.

3. Introduction

Your first paragraph is your introduction. It might be three to four sentences and should contain some essential information. First, you should **state who you are and why you're writing.** Let the hiring manager know **how you learned about the position.**

If you spoke or networked with one of its employees, share her name (assuming the employee has good relationships at the company). Finally, you should **make an impactful statement about your qualifications for the position**. You might give a **succinct summary** of those qualifications before delving into them in the body paragraphs.

Some possible openers include the following:

- I was pleased to see your posting for...
- I was excited to see your listing for...
- I'm writing to express my strong interest in...
- I am responding to your job posting on...for...
- I'm writing to express my interest in joining your team.
- I am applying for...
- As an experienced [position], I was excited to find the [position] opportunity with your organization.

While the above lines can work well, you might also think outside the box and **start your letter in a creative way.** You could start with a story or some sort of personal connection to the organization. Here are a few examples of unconventional cover letter starters:

- When I tried Instacart for the first time last month, I thought I'd died and gone to grocery store shopping heaven. I've been raving about the company to friends and family ever since, so I thought I should make it official by joining your company as your next Community Manager.

- For as long as I can remember, Friday nights meant dinner at Windward. Windward has long been a family favorite due to its amazing food, comfortable atmosphere, and friendly staff. As I take my first steps into the restaurant industry, I'd be thrilled to join your team and treat customers with the same hospitality and care that I've always enjoyed.
- My last boss told me I could probably hold a conversation with a tree (which I took as a compliment). Conversing easily with people from all walks of life has always been a major strength of mine, and it's one that I'd bring to the role of Sales Professional with Match.com.

You should probably **steer clear of tired phrases** that sound pompous or overbearing. For instance, a line like, "If you're looking for an organized, driven worker with great communication skills, then LOOK NO FURTHER" might not make the best of impressions.

Once you've gotten your introduction sorted out, you should indicate **where you learned about the position** in the first sentence.

- I learned about this opportunity from..
- I came across this opportunity on..
- I've been interested in your organization for several years and recently saw that you had an opening for a [position] on your website.
- I've been interested in joining your company for a long time, so I periodically check the open positions listed on your website.

Finally, you might briefly **summarize your qualifications** for the opportunity. You could give an overview of your skills or simply set up what you'll discuss in the rest of the letter. Here are a couple examples:

- I would bring to this position...

- As a [profession] with [#] years of experience, I have the skills and experiences to excel in this role.
- Please allow me to highlight my skills and experiences as they relate to your stated requirements.

Now that you have a sense of what should go into the introduction of your cover letter, let's put all these pieces together with a few examples. Below you'll find **three examples of cover letter introductions,** one for the position of speech language pathologist, another for a web designer, and the third for a software salesperson.

Cover Letter Introduction: Three Examples

Example 1: I was pleased to see your posting for a Speech Language Pathologist (position #357) on SchoolSpring.com. I will be earning my Master's degree in Speech Language Pathology from Boston University this May, and I have extensive experience working in schools with students in grades K through 8. I would bring to this position strong clinical skill, fluency in Mandarin, and a demonstrated commitment to serving young learners.

Example 2: I was excited to see your listing for a front-end web designer on your website. Sun-star has great appeal to me because of its mission to make solar energy affordable to the average consumer. As an experienced web designer who's committed to living a sustainable life, I have both the technical skills and personal passion to excel in this role.

Example 3: I'm writing to express my strong interest in joining Voxacorp's sales team, an opportunity I discovered on Monster.com. With my five years of experience in software sales, I possess the skills and knowledge to excel in this role. Please allow me to highlight my qualifications as they related to your stated requirements.

You can consider the main part of your cover letter to be your argument for why you'd be right for the job. Aim for enthusiasm over aggression, though.

Argument: 2-3 Paragraphs

The body of your cover letter is typically **two to three paragraphs.** Two is usually best, unless you're applying for an especially advanced or specialized type of job. Your cover letter shouldn't go over one page, so two paragraphs usually hits the mark.

You might choose to use **bullet points** here, rather than traditional paragraphs. To give you a sense of how to do this effectively, the third example below is presented in list form. If you're applying for a position that involves a lot of writing, though, then you should probably steer clear of bullet points. This format won't give the hiring manager much insight into your writing skills.

There are a few different ways to format the argument portion of your cover letter, but they should all share the same mission: to **reflect the employer's top needs and explain how you match them** in terms of your skills, knowledge, and experiences.

Here's where the STAR approach (Situation, Task, Action, Result) described earlier come into play. Depending on the position, specific examples that incorporate **data can be useful here.** Presenting specific numbers about your sales record or number of accounts you manage, to give two examples, that measure your achievements could make a strong impression.

In the argument part of your cover letter, consider ways that you can **go beyond your resume points,** personalize your candidacy, and tell a story about who you are and what you'd bring to the job. Present your most relevant experiences and points first. Below are three examples of body paragraphs for the same positions as above, Speech Language Pathologist, Web Designer, and Software Sales Professional.

Body Paragraphs: 3 Examples

Example 1: During my internship at the Briar Middle School in Salem, I created and adapted activities to address students' specific functional needs, including receptive and expressive language skills, articulation, and social pragmatics. To give one example, I worked with a first grade boy throughout the year on pre-literacy and phonological awareness skills. We used reading, oral motor and explicit phonics activities, along with computer assisted instruction. I relied on my coworkers and current research to determine how I could best help him and consistently collected data and reviewed his progress. By the end of the year, his letter-sound correspondence and oral reading skills had greatly improved.

Example 2: As an experienced web designer, I have the technological and design skills that you described in your job posting. I'm fluent in CSS, HTML, and JavaScript and have expertise with Word Press and Word Press plugins. Recently, I designed the main pages for the sustainable clothing company, Oak Tree Co. One major project I worked on was the company's central logo. I reflected Oak Tree's aesthetic of stylish sustainability in the logo it now uses across its site, social media channels, and newsletters. As a web designer with Sun-Star, I would similarly create text and graphic content with visual appeal and a cohesive corporate identity.

Closing Paragraph

The body paragraphs are the most challenging part of your cover letter. Once you've finished them, you can sum everything up with a **concise concluding paragraph.**

In your conclusion, you might restate your interest in the position. Let the employer know if you attached your resume or any other documents, like reference letters. Let them know **when and how to contact you.**

Some professional's advice applicants to **end proactively with a statement about what you'll do next** to continue pursuing the position. Rather than just telling the employer how to get in touch with you, you could say that you plan to contact them in the next few days. You might say you'll call the following week to set up a meeting or discuss the opportunity further. Of course, you have to make sure you get in touch when you said you would!

However, a word of caution about this approach. Some hiring managers **might perceive this call to action as pushy**, even aggressive. You especially should avoid it if application instructions explicitly say, "No calls." **Prioritize the application instructions first and foremost.** Then consider whether the company is one that would appreciate this forward approach or would be turned off by it.

As with all aspects of your cover letter, be thoughtful about your conclusion. It's your **last chance to make a strong impression.** Below are a few examples of closing paragraphs for our example candidates. After your conclusion, you should add "Sincerely" and sign and print your name. If you didn't include it in the header, then you could add your phone number and email under your name.

Closing Paragraph: 3 Examples

Example 1: My clinical skills and experience in educational settings make me well qualified to serve as a Speech Language Pathologist to youth at Lafayette Middle School. As someone who shares Lafayette's commitment to social justice and equity in education, I would be thrilled to join the educational team. I look forward to discussing this position with you and can be reached by phone or email anytime. Thank you very much for your time.

Example 2: As an experienced designer and committed environmentalist, I could bring great value to Sun-Star in the role of web designer. I have attached my resume and hope you will not hesitate to contact me at 999999999 or xyz@gmail.com to arrange a meeting. Thank you for your consideration, and I look forward to meeting with you.

Example 3: My skills and experiences as software sales professional make me well qualified to join the Voxacorp sales team. I would be thrilled to join such an innovative and forward-thinking company. Please

> don't hesitate to contact me, and I will call you on Monday to see about arranging a meeting. Thank you for your consideration. I look forward to speaking with you.

Once you've written your conclusion and signed your name, you should spend some time editing for clarity and proofreading for errors. Now that you have a sense of each piece of your cover letter, let's put them all together into the **final cover letter template!**

Pay attention to little details, like spacing and word choice, to make sure your cover letter looks great.

Final Cover Letter Template

As you saw above, most cover letters share a certain structure. At the same time, you can do a lot to **personalize your letter and inject your own personality.** This template can help steer your writing, but it's your job to consider the best content and format to use to make an authentic impression!

If you're sending your cover letter as an **attachment or hard copy**, then you should include your contact information, the hiring manager's contact information, and the date at the top. Additionally, you could choose a traditional font, like Times New Roman or Garamond in a 12-point size. The template below reflects this traditional format.

If you're pasting your letter into the body of an email or a website's text box, then **don't worry about this formatting.** In these cases, you could start right in with the salutation.

Check out the final cover letter template below, and then scroll down for some **final tips** on producing a great cover letter that will land you that coveted first job interview.

Your Name
Your Address
Phone number and email (optional)

Date

Contact Person
Title
Department
Company or Organization
Address

Dear (Contact Person):

Introduction: 3 - 4 sentences: I'm writing to express my strong interest in joining [organization]'s team in the position of [job title]. I learned of this opportunity from my close friend and [organization name] manager, [name of contact]. I would bring to this position [two to three main skills]. Please allow me to give three examples of my qualifications as they relate to your stated requirements.

Argument: 2-3 paragraphs: As a [profession] with [#] years of experience, I have experience with [skills, knowledge, qualifications]. To give one example...

The body paragraphs should reflect the employer's needs and how your skills, knowledge, and experiences match up with them. If applicable, try to use specific data here.

Closing paragraph: I've attached my resume to give you more information about my professional background. I'm excited to learn more about this opportunity. You can contact me at 5555555555 or myname@gmail.com. Thank you for your consideration, and I look forward to hearing from you.

Sincerely,

[Signature]

Printed name
Phone number*
Email*

*If not present in header

As you saw above, there are several different ways you can phrase your skills and qualifications, and some people choose to present all or most of the body paragraphs in **bullet point or list form**. As long as you follow general guidelines, you have a good amount of wiggle room in the body of your letter.

Above all, you should focus on communicating a sense of professionalism, competence, and cultural fit. In closing, read on for some **final tips** about writing a cover letter for your next job application!

Writing a Cover Letter: Final Tips
Searching for a job can feel like a full-time job in itself, and there's no scarcity of competition. While writing a cover letter can feel like a hurdle in the application

process, you can also see it as **an opportunity to give your candidacy an edge.**

A well-crafted cover letter can catch the reader's attention and **differentiate you from other applicants.** It goes beyond the resume to personalize your application, show your professionalism, and flesh out your qualifications and experiences.

The tone you use may vary depending on the position you're applying for. Some start-ups or creative industries expect a more conversational tone, while more traditional jobs may seek a formal style. Regardless of the approach you take, you should make sure to **express enthusiasm for the opportunity and the organization.**

A strong letter shows your writing skills, attention to detail, and understanding of the employer's needs. If you're serious about a job, **take the time to craft a concise, persuasive argument** that proves you're the best person for the job.

SAMPLE COVER LETTERS

Your Name
142 Your Address
Your City, State, xxxxx United States
(xxx)xxx-xxxx
your.email@gmail.com

[Today's Date]
[Hiring Manager's Name]

[341 Company Address
Company City, State, xxxxx
(xxx)xxx-xxxx
hiring.manager@gmail.com]

Dear Mr./Mrs./Ms. [Manager's Name],

This email is in regards to my interest in applying for the (POSITION) recently posted on (website). With my skill-set and competencies I am more than able to investigate several forensic examination processes and monitor security systems for multiple fortune 500 companies.

While pursuing an Associate Degree in Information Security and Digital Forensics from Trident Community College, I have developed skills in reverse engineering, computer forensics, networking and information security. This knowledge has enabled me to operate in Windows and Linux platforms and master multiple security principles.

I started my career as an Information Security Intern with Chicago Government in May 2011. Working under the direction of senior members, I monitored the overall security of the system and investigated likely loopholes. Utilizing my academic and professional knowledge, I dedicated two years with Technology Smart while working in the capacity of Network Operations Center Monitoring Technician. Here I gained an opportunity to work in a Datacenter environment, improve existing documentation systems and implement stringent measures to improve the overall network security.

I currently work as a Security Operations Center Security Analyst with Security Professionals Inc., where I have been able to further strengthen my technical acumen. I have attached my resume highlighting my academic and professional skills and look forward to hearing from you in due course.

Sincerely,
[Name]

[Information Technology Cover Letter]

COVER LETTER TEMPLATE

Your Details
Name
Address
Contact Number
Email Address

Date

Employer Details
Company Name
Recruiter and Job Title
Address
Phone, Fax, Email

Dear_____.

Re: Job Title and Job ID

Paragraph 1 – Reason

I am applying for the above position you have advertised in the Herald Sun on the 23rd July 2009.

Paragraph 2 – Interest

- Why are you applying for the position? Do you have the skills, experience or qualities and qualifications required to fill the position?
- Why are you interested in the position and the company?

Paragraph 3 – Persuasion

Refer to your resume and provide more details about the skills and experience that you have to offer. Prove or explain why you are suitable for the position (you may give some short examples or refer to previous experience/positions).

Paragraph 4 – Action and Closing

State what you believe will occur next. Also prove that you are keen by stating that you look forward to having an interview. Sign off with 'Regards', or 'Kind Regards', followed by you signature and name.

Please find my resume attached for your further reference. I look forward to having the opportunity to discuss my application further and am available for an interview any time.
Thank you for your time and consideration of my application.

Kind Regards,

(Sign here)

Print your name

YOUR NAME

123 Four Street • City 10110 • 123.456.7890
you@email.com • www.linkedin.com/yourname.com

[Date]
[Recipient Name]
[Title]
[Company Name]
[Street Address]
[Address 2]
[City, ST ZIP Code]

Dear [Recipient Name]:

Upon review of the job description for the [Title] role at [Company Name], I was excited about the opportunity to leverage my subject matter expertise to support the organization's financial management endeavors. With over fifteen years of hands-on experience, I have gained a great deal of knowledge that is applicable to this position including client relationship management, underwriting, loan administration, market research and data analysis.

As noted in my resume, I have several years of experience in the banking industry; all of my previous roles necessitated refined business acumen and strategic business development expertise. Throughout my career I leveraged a diverse skill set including marketing, revenue generation and relationship cultivation to ensure organizational success. I also have led process improvement initiatives; as a Senior Loan Specialist I implemented procedures that altered the branch's stature from below average to a top performing location within 90 days. I am committed to providing quality service to my employer and working diligently toward overarching goals.

I am confident that my skill set and professional expertise uniquely position me as a viable candidate for this role. I look forward to meeting you to further discuss the [Title] role at [Company Name].

Sincerely,

Your Name

CHAPTER-7

How to Write Resume Employers Will Notice

How can you make your resume stand out to potential employers? There are a few guidelines to follow that can help your resume shine. Better still; a winning resume may encourage employers to contact you about job opportunities. In fact, 1.7 million employers use the Indeed Resume database to search for qualified candidate

In this article, we'll share what employers look for in a resume, how to describe your work experience and proofreading tips to make your resume shine.

What employers look for in a resume?

Your resume is often your first and best chance to get noticed by recruiters and hiring managers. Your goal is to make it easy for them to see that you have the qualifications they're looking for.

Often, employers have several core skills that they want candidates to demonstrate. Because they may be reading through hundreds of applications, a recruiter or hiring manager might quickly scan your resume to see if those qualifications jump out.

It's also important to note that online job applications are often sorted through software called an applicant tracking system. This software scans resumes and cover letters for relevant experience, skills and other keywords so that qualified candidates are easy for employers to identify. Employers will use those same keywords when they proactively search for candidates.

Follow these guidelines to write a resume that's easy for employers to find and read:

- Read job descriptions closely to identify required skills and experience. You may want to make a list of the requirements you see. Refer back to this list as you're writing your resume. If you have these skills, list them prominently (more tips on this below). If you don't meet the exact requirements, list your related or similar skills. For example, if a job description asks for three to five years of experience and you have two years, write "2+ years of experience in [your job or industry]." If you don't have the required skills and experience, you may want to refine your job search to find a good match.

- Use a simple format. This means leading with contact information (your name, email address, phone number and the city where you live), followed by an optional summary, your work experience, skills and education. Complicated page layouts can be hard for applicant tracking systems to handle.

- Use a standard font. Arial, Calibri and Georgia are good options. Use 10, 11 or 12 point font.

- For most resumes, it's best to keep it to two pages maximum. Carefully consider if everything you've included is necessary.

How to write your resume headline or summary (with examples)

Beginning your resume with a headline or summary statement (sometimes known as a resume objective) is one way to clearly callout your most relevant qualifications. This short description should quickly advertise your skill set and professional goals to any reader.

A headline is the shortest version: sum up your achievements in one line. In a summary or objective statement, you can get a little longer: one or two sentences is typically a good length.

To get started, think back on your proudest career accomplishments and what defines who you are in the workplace. Carefully read the job descriptions that you're considering. Do they require a specific certification or years of experience? Your headline is the place to let the employer know you meet these requirements.

For example, a customer service representative with a track record of customer satisfaction might write: Customer success professional with 3+ years' experience delighting clients in the retail industry.

Similarly, an experienced dental assistant could write: Certified dental assistant with 12+ years in direct patient care.

The above are both great examples of engaging and descriptive headlines. If you want, you can pair that with a slightly longer summary of your skills and career goals. Here are a few examples:

Example 1

- Headline: **Customer success professional with 3+ years' experience delighting clients in the retail industry.**
- Summary: Experienced in resolving client concerns via chat, email and phone; routinely recognized by management and peers for assertive and enthusiastic spirit. Excited to continue my career in ecommerce.

Example 2

- Headline: **Certified dental assistant with 12+ years in direct patient care.**
- Summary: Extensive experience in charting, scheduling and delivering best in class customer service. Vast knowledge of clinical procedure and dental terminology. Looking for new opportunities in private dental practice.

Example 3

- Headline: **Aspiring financial services professional with degree in Business Administration.**
- Summary: Advanced Excel and intermediate SQL skills, excellent written and verbal communication, pursuing entry-level roles in financial services.

Example 4

- Headline: **Graphic designer with strong experience as creative lead in an agency setting.**
- Summary: Mastery of Adobe Creative Cloud and familiarity with Sketch, InVision, HTML, CSS and Javascript.

How to write out your work experience

Once you've written your resume summary, the next section to take on is your work experience. (Note: in some cases, your education may be listed before your work experience. Today, it's more common for education to come at the end of the resume, though it depends on your industry and when you received your education. We'll cover education further down.)

Listing out your experience is not as simple as writing down everything you've done in your career. Instead, you want to only include the details of your past work that are especially relevant to the work you want to do next.

Follow these guidelines to list out your work experience so employers can quickly understand your background:

- Use bullet points rather than paragraphs. Writing out your experience in a list has the double benefit of using fewer words and making it easier for employers to read.
- Lead with **strong action verbs** and follow with an accomplishment rather than a task. Employers are interested in what you've achieved, not just what you've done. What's the difference between an accomplishment and a task? Here are a few examples:

    Task: Greeted customers
    Accomplishment: Provided friendly

and helpful service by greeting customers.

Task: Analyzed marketing campaign performance
Accomplishment: Reported on ROI of marketing campaigns, improving campaign efficiency by 20%.

Task: Took patient vitals and updated charts
Accomplishment: Performed routine clinical procedures while ensuring patient comfort and updating charts via an EMR system.

- Add quantifiable results whenever possible. This helps employers better understand your contributions. For example, an operations manager might write, "Identified and implemented supply chain improvements which decreased fulfillment costs by 17%." Similarly, a retail sales associate might say, "Regularly evaluated showroom inventory and refreshed displays with stock, increasing daily sales by 22%.

Not every bullet point on your resume will have a quantifiable result. For everything you include, however, ask yourself if there is an applicable number that can help potential employers see your achievements clearly.

- Include more details about your most recent jobs and fewer details from roles you held earlier in your career. If you have many years of experience, it's reasonable to only include information from the last 10 to 15 years. Employers are most likely to be interested in your current accomplishments.
- If you can, fill employment gaps with other experiences such as education or freelance work. Did you take classes, earn any certifications or volunteer during the time you weren't formally employed? If you worked on personal projects or as a freelancer, you can put "Self-employed" where you would otherwise list an employer. The same guidelines about how to write out your accomplishments apply here, too.

What to include in the education section

These days, it's common for education to be listed at the end of your resume. Exceptions to this may be if you're applying for jobs that require specific certifications (as in the healthcare industry, for example), or if you are a recent graduate.

In the education section of your resume, list all of the relevant degrees or certifications that make you qualified for this job. If you have attained a degree, list your degree type and field of study followed by the name of your educational institution and the city and state. List honors, if you have them. You don't need to include your GPA, especially if it's under 3.5. Unless you're a recent graduate, you don't need to list your graduation date. For example:

B.A. in History
University of Arizona, Tuscon, AZ
Honors: *magna cum laude*

A.A.S. in Cardiac Sonography
Bunker Hill Community College, Boston, MA
Honors: Dean's list

If you have multiple degrees, list your highest level of education first.

If you have attended a program of study but didn't graduate, you can list the years you attended and the credits you received. For example:

Indiana State University, Terre Haute, IN 2010-2012; Completed 75 credits towards a Bachelor's in Business Administration

If you are currently in a program of study, you can list the degree you're pursuing and your expected graduation date. If you're still in school and applying for internships, potential employers may want to know your GPA. For example:

B.S. in Computer Science, degree anticipated May 2020
Harvey Mudd College, Claremont, CA
GPA: 3.8

What to include in your skills section

In your skills section, you want to list the skills you have that make you qualified for the jobs you're applying for. Employers will indicate the skill sets they are looking for in their job descriptions. Look closely at the posting, and if you have the required skills be sure to list them.

In general, there are two types of skills: soft skills and hard skills. Soft skills include things like interpersonal communication, organization or attention to detail. Hard skills are more often tied to specific tools, software or knowledge (speaking a foreign language, for example). Hard skills will vary by industry or job type while soft skills tend to be more universal.

You can list your skills in a single paragraph with each skill separated by a comma. Start with the skills you're most proficient in. You may choose to call out your levels of mastery, for example:

Advanced in Excel, Quickbooks, ProSystems. Some familiarity with SAP and Checkpoint.

Pro-tip: If you're applying for a job where a specific skill is often taken for granted, don't list it. For many jobs, one example is Microsoft Office. Instead, focus on proficiencies within that skill. For instance, instead of listing "Microsoft Office," you could list "Macros, pivot tables and vlookups" if you know how to do these things in Excel.

Proofreading your resume

After taking the time to write a great resume, you don't want typos and spelling mistakes to get in the way of submitting a winning application. Reread your resume from top to bottom and then from bottom to top, correcting mistakes as you find them. It's also a good idea to ask a friend or family member to read it for you — they will look at it with fresh eyes and may find mistakes more readily.

SOME SAMPLE RESUME

Curriculum Vitae

XYZ
Address:
Mobile :

Photo

Objective

Clothing designer with industry experience in womens, mens and childrenswear. Highly self motivated and results driven. Take a keen interest in current trends and have a passion for all things fashion and clothing related.

Fast and effective. I want to be a part of your success by offering high motivation, responsibility, quality work and keeping deadlines. I'm working with following software: Wilcom es 1.5,Melco design shop v9, Corel Draw X6, Adobe Photoshop CS6.1, Adobe Illustrator CS5. I'm using high quality fonts for modern design.

Education

Exam	:	**B. Sc. in Textile Engineering**
Session	:	2011-2012
Institution	:	The People's University of Bangladesh, Dhaka
Status	:	Fashion & Design
Exam	:	**National Skill Standard Basic (Graphics Design)**
Session	:	2011
Board	:	Bangladesh Technical Education Board, Dhaka
Result	:	A+
Exam	:	**Diploma in Textile Engineering**
Board	:	Dhaka
Session	:	2006-2009
Institution	:	Pabna Textile Engineering College
Result	:	A
Exam	:	**SSC**
Board	:	Dhaka
Session	:	2006
Institution	:	Textile Vocational Institute, Kushtia
Result	:	A

Computer Skill

- Design Application (Wilcom es 1.5, Melco design shop v9, Corel Draw X6, Adobe Photoshop CS6, Adobe Illustrator CS5, AutoCAD)
- Experienced in Windows 98, Windows XP, Windows 7, Windows 8 OS environment
- Office Applications (MS Word, MS Excel, MS Access, MS PowerPoint, MS Outlook).
- Internet: Blogging, Website Making, SEO, SMM, Browsing & E mail literacy.
- Hardware & Software Troubleshooting.
   -Trained by *Path Finder Computer Training Institute, Pabna*

Language Proficiency

Good command over English & colloquial Bengali.

xyz

Address　　　　　Mobile

CAREER OBJECTIVE

Administrative Assistant with 6+ years of experience working directly for the President of 3M Inc., a Fortune 500 company. Possesses impeccable written and verbal communication skills and excellent interpersonal skills.

CORE COMPETENCIES

- Customer Service
- Cost Efficient
- Detailed and Organized
- Supplier Relationship

PROFESSIONAL EXPERIENCE

3M INC., New York, NY
Administrative Assistant, Apr 2006 – present
- Read and analyze incoming memos, submissions, and reports to determine their significance and plan their distribution.
- Conduct research, compile data, and prepare papers for consideration and presentation by executives, committees and boards of directors.
- Coordinate and direct office services, such as records, departmental finances, budget preparation, personnel issues, and housekeeping, to aid executives.
- Prepare invoices, reports, memos, letters, financial statements and other documents, using word processing, spreadsheet, database, or presentation software.

FLORIDA DEPARTMENT OF SOCIAL SERVICES, Orlando, FL
Rehabilitation Counselor, Aug 2004 – May 2006
- Confer with clients to discuss their options and goals so that rehabilitation programs and plans for accessing needed services can be developed.
- Prepare and maintain records and case files, including documentation such as clients' personal and eligibility information, services provided, narratives of client contacts, and relevant correspondence.
- Develop and maintain relationships with community referral sources, such as schools and community groups.
- Analyze information from interviews, educational and medical records, consultation with other professionals, and diagnostic evaluations to assess clients' abilities, needs, and eligibility for services.

EDUCATION

FLORIDA STATE UNIVERSITY, Orlando, FL
Bachelor of Art in English, May 2004
- GPA: 3.3/4.0
- Published in school's newspaper editorial
- Summer Internship for the New York Times

ADDITIONAL SKILLS

- Proficient in Microsoft Office and Adobe Illustrator CS5
- Bilingual Spanish and English
- Employee of the Month for 3 consecutive months in H&M
- Won the "Writer's Digest" 2002 Award
- Awarded an employee travel award due to "Performance Excellence" 2 years in a row through 3M Inc.

Address:
Mobile:

MARKETING EXECUTIVE

Product Launches ~ Overseas Partnerships ~ Presentations

Accomplished, multilingual Professional consistently recognized for achievement and performance in the fuel industry. Innovative and successful in mining new sales territories and establishing business alliances, including the recent partnership with MJM Oil in Korea. Proven leader with special capabilities in building teams, strategizing, and implementing workable marketing plans employing television, radio, Internet, and print media. Fluent in English, Korean, Japanese, and French.

BUSINESS SKILLS

Marketing

- Launch gasoline exports in conjunction with new production plant start-up; target overseas markets.
- Initiate sales of ULS, an environmentally-friendly new product launched in the European market.
- Establish joint venture partnerships in Europe and Far East; implement marketing for aviation fuel and asphalt as a value-added commodity.

Market Planning

- Analyze regional import / export economics and the interregional oil markets.
- Participate in contract negotiations for strategic alliances with major European and Asian concerns.
- Achieved $25 million in revenue by developing offshore storage programs that fulfilled seasonal market trends in the region.

Product Planning

- Optimize production mode by selecting appropriate refinery; research product specification revisions by country.
- Propose and participate in the Plant Operation Committee, a team effort between production and sales.

PROFESSIONAL EXPERIENCE

TTR CORPORATION, New York, New York   1993 – Present
Vice President, Overseas Business Division
- Promoted to position in March 1996; selected as one of three employees to attend an MBA course in 2003.
- Named *Employee of the Year* in 1996 based on professional achievements.

FUEL INDUSTRY OF AMERICA, New York, New York   1989 – 1992
Manager of Marketing
- Provided analysis on fuel industry; drafting report for the White House.
- Awarded the *Honor Prize* in 1992 based on performance evaluations of oil producers.

EDUCATION

UNIVERSITY OF NEW YORK, New York, New York
Bachelor of Arts in Communications, 1988

xyz

Cell Phone #:
Email address:

Photo

CARRER OBJECTIVE

I am seeking for company where my experience can not only improve the status of the company but also automate the working process to the best possible one.

PERSONAL INFORMATION

Date of Birth: April 18, 1990
Age: 22   **Civil Status:** Single
Nickname: Jean, Emjhay
Mother: Rona Macasinag
Father: Junisil Macasinag
Religion: Christian Born Again

Place of Birth: Manila
Position Desired: Manager
Gender: Female
Occupation: Housewife
Occupation: Driver

EDUCATIONAL ATTAINMENT

Tertiary Education
School: Universidad De Manila
Degree: B.S. Education, Major in Biology Science
Address: Arocerros Mehan Garden, Manila
School Year: 2006- 2012

Secondary Education
School: LakanDula High School
Address: Gagalangin, Manila
School Year: 2002-2006

Elementary School
School: Dr. Jose Rizal Elementary School
Address: Tayuman, Manila
School Year: 1997-2002

WORK EXPERIENCE:

NSTP PROGRAM practice teaching
Daycare Center Pandacan
135 hours

Practice Teaching
Cayetano Arellano High School
630 hours

www.ingramcontent.com/pod-product-compliance
Lightning Source LLC
Chambersburg PA
CBHW031925240526
45464CB00022B/878